RELEASE *Your Words*

IMPACT *Your World*

DARRELL PARSONS

I0809562

Parsons Publishing House
Your Voice Your World™

RELEASE YOUR WORDS – IMPACT YOUR WORLD
by Darrell J. Parsons
Parsons Publishing House
P. O. Box 6428
Panama City, FL 32404
www.ParsonsPublishingHouse.com
Info@ParsonsPublishingHouse.com

Cover Design by Brian Banashak
Genesis Communications.

International Standard Book Number:
13 digit: 978-1-60273-000-7
10 digit: 1-60273-000-8
Library of Congress Control Number: 2007901439
Printed in the United States of America.

ENDORSEMENT

Darrell Parsons clearly articulates the importance and responsibility that every believer has to release what God has put within them. He points out that God has given every Christian a word that can and should be shared with others that He has called them to influence. He further emphasizes the necessity to act on what has been deposited within us and not allow procrastination to rob us from God's best for our lives. This is not just a message that Darrell writes about, it is one that he has lived. I highly recommend this well written book. It will be an inspiration and encouragement to all who read it to RELEASE YOUR WORDS.

— Pastor Robert Gay
High Praise Worship Center
Panama City, Florida USA

ACKNOWLEDGMENTS

First and foremost, I would like to acknowledge my thanks and dependency on my Lord Jesus. Without Him, I would be hopelessly and eternally lost and without a voice. With Him, I can do all things.

I am thankful to God for my loving wife Diane and my beautiful daughter Brianna. They are truly the apple of my eye and the joy of my life. With my wife and daughter beside me, I feel like a champion everyday.

It is with the deepest honor and respect that I have to be counted among the many that Dr. Myles Munroe has mentored over the years.

If you listen closely to this book, you will hear his words resounding throughout.

My heartfelt thanks to Dr. Ron Kenoly for his faithfulness and dedication to my family. We have had many adventures together and I look forward to many more.

I have been blessed with the covering of my church, High Praise Worship Center, and my pastors, Robert and Stacey Gay. Without their unselfish love and support, these words may never have been heard. My church family has been unparalleled in their support for my family and this venture. I am a better person and a better Christian because of their influence in my life.

TABLE OF CONTENTS

FOREWORD
BY DR. RON KENOLY

Day after day, average people work towards completing tasks and assignments in an effort to make their lives better or make money for someone else. Many of their efforts seem to go unnoticed and their accomplishments frequently go unrewarded.

The songwriter Oscar Hammerstein wrote in his song "Ol' Man River," that we have to tote that barge and lift that bale; sometimes, we get tired of living and sick of trying. Millions of people see no sign of an end to the struggles and hardships of life. Millions of people see their lives as a meaningless existence. They face each day without a sense of passion or direction. Are there any answers to these issues in the lives of so many? Is there any rest for the weary? Where is the joy that makes life worth living? What is the purpose for my life? Am I supposed to go on like this forever?

The answers to these questions and more can be found in the word of God. There is a dynamic plan and a specific purpose for every life that God has created. God expects us to live an abundant and prosperous life filled with joy and victory. He not only expects us to do great things, but He also expects us to pass on to others the written history of our victories and triumphs in Christ.

In his book, Darrell Parsons makes us aware that our lives are more than spaces in the history of time. We are fearfully and wonderfully made for the plans and purposes of our Great Creator. God knows each of us by name and holds us accountable for the gifts, talents, abilities and resources that He has deposited in us.

Through visions, dreams, revelations, and inspirations, we are able to see clearly the plan of God for our lives. The Bible tells us to write down the vision so that we may remain focused on what He has called us to do.

Write the vision, draft the plan, schedule the process and document the success. The Bible is a record of all of these things. It is our operations manual for this life and the life to come. The Bible was written to help us attain eternal life and sustain us in this present stage of our existence.

We have all been blessed to have a word and a testimony. Darrell Parsons encourages us to write our words and our testimonies. Our writings could be the tools and equipment that cut the trail and smooth the rough road for our children and our children's children.

Dr. Ron Kenoly
Worship Leader & Teacher
Orlando, Florida USA

INTRODUCTION

Ecclesiastes 3:1
To everything there is a season, a time for every purpose under heaven.

All the wisdom of Solomon can be captured in Ecclesiastes 3:1. There is a season for every thing and every purpose has a time.

NOW is the TIME and PURPOSE for your season.

God has looked down from heaven and decreed that it is time for your purpose to be revealed. How do I know? The Lord has instructed and impressed me to write this book for you. You are not holding this book by accident! You did not pick it up by chance!

The Lord God of Heaven and Earth has guided you to this book at this time in your life. Why? Your season is NOW and it is time for your purpose to be revealed. For you see, the plan and purpose of God has not been hidden FROM you, but is has been hidden FOR you! It was a great day in my life when I realized this truth. Now is your time and this is your season. The enemy may be walking about as a roaring lion in your life, but he has already been defeated.

> *John 10:10*
> *The thief does not come except to steal, and to kill, and to destroy. I have come that they may have life, and that they may have it more abundantly.*

There is a real enemy and his purpose is to steal, kill and destroy your voice! However, Jesus has come to give life to your voice and to give purpose to your life. In the original Greek language of the New Testament, the word translated "steal" is the Greek word *kleptoo*, which is where we get the word "kleptomaniac". It also means to take away by stealth.

When we choose NOT to write and publish the voice that God has given us, we are allowing stealth to remove the voice of God from the earth. It is time to be silent no longer! Do not allow stealth to take away or destroy your voice from the earth.

To "destroy" means to perish, to be lost, ruined and destroyed forever. God has given you a voice, a revelation, and an anointing that He does not want to be lost, ruined, or destroyed forever.

Further study shows the word "life" comes from the Greek word *zoe* which means the absolute fullness of life or the God-kind of life. Jesus came to give us the absolute fullness of life in abundance. Now, He wants us to give out to others all that He has poured into us.

Freely we receive and freely we give. The Lord desires to release His voice through your voice TODAY! Now is the time.

THIS IS THE SEASON TO RELEASE YOUR WORDS AND IMPACT YOUR WORLD!

Books Will Speak Plain When Counsellors Blanch

Bacon, Essays "Of Counsel"

Glory Is Acquired By Virtue But Preserved By Letters

Petrarch

The Chief Glory of Every People Arises From Its Authors

Johnson, Preface, A Dictionary of the English Language

Reading Maketh A Full Man; Conference A Ready Man; And Writing, An Exact Man

Bacon, Essays, "Of Studies"

CHAPTER ONE

FROM HERE TO ETERNITY

Ecclesiastes 3:11
He has made everything beautiful in its time. Also He has put eternity in their hearts.

Seasons come and seasons go. Life is full of seasons. Our God wants your life to be complete with seasons of absolute abundance. As the Lord has poured His revelation and anointing into your life, He wants you to allow that anointing or unction to flow through you for generations to come. Your anointing begins here, but will last into eternity.

The plan and purpose God has ordained for your life is not just for now, but it is forever.

God has put eternity in your heart. The Creator of the Universe has given you an anointing that will abide forever. Not only will you live forever with Him, but His intention is that your anointing and your purpose will live forever.

The great teacher and scholar, Dr. Myles Munroe, has said the richest place in the world is the graveyard because of all of the unpublished books and unwritten songs that are lost forever. These things should not be! The graveyard is not the eternity that God intends for your purpose.

Do not let your epitaph be, "Here lie the greatest books, greatest songs, and best ideas of all mankind."

Now is the time and this is the season! Eternity is waiting for you. The entire Earth is groaning and waiting for what the God of the Universe has to say through you. The Lord gave you a voice that counts. Your voice is important!

> *1 Thessalonians 1:8*
> *For from you the word of the Lord has sounded forth, not only in Macedonia and Achaia, but also in every place.*

God has placed His voice – His word - in you and He wants it to be heard throughout His

Kingdom. The enemy - the devil - would like nothing better than to silence your voice. He may have told you that you have nothing to say and that you are unimportant. Jesus has your answer for the lies of the enemy concerning your plan, purpose and voice.

> *John 8:44-45*
> *You are of your father the devil, and the desires of your father you want to do. He was a murderer from the beginning, and does not stand in the truth, because there is no truth in him. When he speaks a lie he speaks from his own resources, for he is a liar and the father of it.*

The enemy is nothing but a liar and the father of all lies.

Evangelist R.W. Shambach says it best when he retorts with his loud trademark teaching, "The devil is a liar!" So when the enemy tells you that you are defeated, remember that he is a liar. When the enemy tells you that you have nothing to say, remember that he is a liar. You do have something to say and now IS the time to say it.

The Apostle Paul is known for writing over half of the New Testament. It is not as well-known that the majority of his writing was done while he was imprisoned. What the devil meant for evil, God turned for good.

Paul could have easily become discouraged in his walk with the Lord. He was beaten, put in chains, shipwrecked and even thrown in jail. In the end, however, Paul was neither discouraged nor dismayed; he was strong in faith.

> *2 Timothy 4:6-8*
> *For I am already being poured out as a drink offering, and the time of my departure is at hand. I have fought the good fight, I have finished the race, I have kept the faith. Finally, there is laid up for me the crown of righteousness, which the Lord, the righteous Judge, will give to me on that Day, and not to me only but also to all who have loved His appearing.*

Paul not only proclaimed that he fought the good fight and kept the faith, but he also wrote it down to be read by all who came after him. His words are recorded forever because they were written down and made public.

The Apostle Paul's words will last for all eternity.

The end of his race was at hand, but he wanted to ensure that all who followed would hear his testimony. Had these words not been recorded and made public, he would have taken them to his grave and never been heard again. The book of Timothy was written while Paul was under "house arrest" in Rome. Even though he was imprisoned, Paul fulfilled his purpose!

You may feel like your words and your influence are in prison. You may feel like your purpose is under "house arrest." At the right time and in the right season, the Lord wants to bring forth the purpose for your voice. At that time, you must be obedient and he will provide a platform to release your voice.

Writing and publishing is that outlet.

If you feel like you are in a dead-end job and your voice is locked inside yourself, I have good news for you. There is a purpose in your "prison." Take this time while you are hidden away and write!

"What shall I write?"

Mark chapter five has your answer. There was a man from the country of the Gadarenes that we've called the Madman from Gadera. This man was imprisoned inside himself with no escape. No purpose. No future.

Mark 5:1-6
Then they came to the other side of the sea, to the country of the Gadarenes. And when He had come out of the boat, immediately there met Him out of the tombs a man with an unclean spirit, who had his dwelling among the tombs; and no one could bind him, not even with chains, because he had often been bound with shackles and chains. And the chains had been pulled apart by him, and the shackles broken in pieces; neither could anyone tame him. And always, night and day, he was in the mountains and in the tombs, crying out and cutting himself with stones. When he saw Jesus from afar, he ran and worshiped Him.

The madman from Gadera is the epitome of being broken, busted and disgusted.

If any man has ever been without hope and without purpose, it was this man. Yet, he had a visitation from Jesus. The Lord was able to look beyond the moment and see the purpose hidden inside of this man. His voice was silent until he had an encounter with Jesus. When he saw Jesus, the madman ran to Him and worshipped Him.

One moment of worship can change your life forever.

One encounter with the Most High is enough to change your destiny forever. It does not matter how silent your voice may have become, one moment with the King will awaken your voice with renewed purpose. When the madman came and worshipped, the demons named "Legion" began to tremble and cry out with a loud voice.

> *Mark 5:7-10*
> *And he cried out with a loud voice and said, "What have I to do with You, Jesus, Son of the Most High God? I implore You by God that You do not torment me." For He said to him, "Come out of the man, unclean spirit!" Then He asked him, "What is your name?" And he answered, saying, "My name is Legion; for we are many." Also he begged Him earnestly that He would not send them out of the country.*

Imagine, demons invoking the name of God in order to be spared from torment! This is why the enemy is determined to silence your voice. Your voice, released under the authority of Jesus, has the power and the ability to torment demons and drive them away. The only defense the enemy has against your voice is to silence you. Refuse to allow the enemy to silence your voice!

Allow your voice to be heard for all eternity.

As you write and publish, your voice is released into eternity. The enemy will try to convince you otherwise, but note that Jesus begins speaking to the demons and directing their future.

> *Mark 5:11-13*
> *Now a large herd of swine was feeding there near the mountains. So all the demons begged Him, saying, "Send us to the swine, that we may enter them." And at once Jesus gave them permission. Then the unclean spirits went out and entered the swine (there were about two thousand); and the herd ran violently down the steep place into the sea, and drowned in the sea.*

The demons were subject to the voice of the Lord. The Bible says that we have been given the authority over all of the power of the evil one (Luke 10:19). As you speak in the Name of Jesus, that same voice resonates throughout

Heaven and Earth with the same authority and power now as it did then!

Without the leading of the Holy Spirit directing Mark to record and publish this story, it would have been lost forever. However, God wanted to impart this truth and principle for future generations. Mark wrote it down and forever settled the authority that believers have when using the Name of Jesus.

Demons tremble at the Name of Jesus.

What happened to the man that was delivered from the Legion of demons?

> *Mark 5:18-20*
> *And when he was come into the ship, he that had been possessed with the devil prayed him that he might be with him. Howbeit Jesus suffered him not, but saith unto him, Go home to thy friends, and tell them how great things the Lord hath done for thee, and hath had compassion on thee. And he departed, and began to publish in Decapolis how great things Jesus had done for him: and all men did marvel. (KJV)*

Verse twenty says that he departed and began to "publish" the great things that Jesus had done for him. Where do you begin? Begin just as this man and publish your testimony. Write down your victories, insights and revelations about the Lord Jesus and living the Christian life for future generations to read.

Publish the great things that God has done for you!

What became of the madman of Gadera who published abroad all that God had done? Jesus returned to the Decapolis area in Mark chapter seven with signs and wonders.

> *Mark 7:31-37*
> *Again, departing from the region of Tyre and Sidon, He came through the midst of the region of Decapolis to the Sea of Galilee. Then they brought to Him one who was deaf and had an impediment in his speech, and they begged Him to put His hand on him. And He took him aside from the multitude, and put His fingers in his ears, and He spat and touched his tongue. Then, looking up to heaven, He sighed, and said to him, "Ephphatha," that is, "Be opened."*
>
> *Immediately his ears were opened, and the impediment of his tongue*

> *was loosed, and he spoke plainly. Then He commanded them that they should tell no one; but the more He commanded them, the more widely they proclaimed it. And they were astonished beyond measure, saying, "He has done all things well. He makes both the deaf to hear and the mute to speak."*

History tells us that a great revival was sparked throughout this ten-city region all because of one man's passion to publish what Jesus had done for him.

PERSONAL REFLECTIONS

Chapter One
From Here to Eternity

1. Seasons come and seasons go. Life is full of different seasons. What season do you think your life is in today?

2. Are you happy with where your life is at today? If so, what steps did you take to get there. If not, what steps can you take to IMPROVE YOUR HAPPINESS IN LIFE?.

3. It has been said that the greatest books, greatest song and best ideas are in the grave because people did not take the time to write and express them. What can you do in order for this not to happen to you?

4. One moment of worship can change your life forever! Describe a time in your life when you needed the presence of God.

5. Mark chapter five relates the story of the madman from Gadera. Have you ever had a season in your life like this man's?

CHAPTER TWO

WRITE THE VISION

Habakkuk 2:2-3
Then the LORD answered me and said, "Write the vision and make it plain on tablets, that he may run who reads it. For the vision is yet for an appointed time; but at the end it will speak."

THE Prophet Habakkuk had many questions for the Lord. God responded by answering his questions. Then He commanded Habakkuk to write those answers down for future generations.

We now have access to Habakkuk's revelation from the Lord because Habakkuk wrote it down.

The book of Habakkuk is not a large book; it has only three chapters and just over 1500 words. Yet, it is a powerful book with a strong prophetic message that will last throughout eternity because Habakkuk followed the Lord's instructions and wrote it down.

Over 2500 years later, we still benefit from the truth and anointing in that book. Habakkuk still speaks today because he wrote it down. If we want future generations to receive from our voice and anointing, then we must follow the same pattern and direction from the Lord.

Write the vision and make it plain!

What about the vision that is in your life? How will you cultivate it? How will it be developed? Where there is no vision, there is no revelation. According to the ***Strong's Exhaustive Concordance***, there are several types of visions in the Bible, all of which are a divine communication.

Our vision must originate from God's vision. In fact, most of the people in the Bible never chose their vision. They simply chose to serve God and He revealed to them their purpose and destiny.

Proverbs 29:18 states that, "Where there is no vision, the people perish." "Perish" is an action verb that means to become unrestrained or to decay from within. In ***The Random House Unabridged Dictionary***, *"perish"* is defined as, " to die or be destroyed; to pass away or disappear." *Perish* means to pass from existence.

A lack of vision is destructive because people are ignorant about what to do.

The famous deaf and blind author and activist Helen Keller once said, "Worse than blindness is sight without vision." Some people lack vision and do not know what to do in their daily lives. Others have a vision of their destiny and are doing nothing about it. Paul instructs us in Ephesians 6:13-14 that "having done all, to stand. Stand therefore." The point here is that we do all we can and then we stand and believe God to accomplish it.

The second law of thermodynamics is the law of entropy. Simply put this means that when all forces are left unattended, they will go from order to chaos. A house which is left unattended deteriorates: the roof leaks and the foundation cracks. The law of entropy applies to things and people. Entropy leads to destruction. Your inactivity leads to your destruction.

The Bible says that God's people perish or are destroyed by two things: a lack of knowledge and a lack of vision. The essence of "knowledge" refers to what has been acquired through study or experience.

> *Hosea 4:6*
> *My people are destroyed for lack of knowledge.*

The ***Strong's Greek and Hebrew Dictionary*** defines "destroyed" as "to be brought to silence, to be undone." Today's definition would also include: to ruin, to tear down or break up, to demolish, to kill and to render useless or ineffective. People are rendered ineffective when they are silent about their vision.

If the enemy can silence your voice, he can destroy you!

In the King James Version, Proverbs 29:18, says, "Where there is no vision, the people perish." People perish for a lack of vision or a lack of activity towards accomplishing their vision. There is a connection between a lack of knowledge and a lack of vision. The converse of that is also true. With knowledge and vision, you will be built up and raised up.

In the spirit realm, knowledge is possession.

If you know it, you can have it. If you want to be a school teacher, go learn how to teach. If you want to be a businessman, go learn about business. If you want to be a writer, learn how to write.

Some have said, "I don't need knowledge; I have the anointing." Wisdom is available to all, but you must choose to be a person of understanding to draw it out.

> *Proverbs 1:20, 22*
> *Wisdom calls aloud outside; she raises her voice in the open squares... For scorner delight in their scorning, and fools hate knowledge.*

Wisdom in not hidden FROM you, it is hidden FOR you.

The Lord has strong words for those who reject knowledge.

> *Proverbs 1:29-33*
> *Because they hated knowledge and did not choose the fear of the LORD, they would have none of my counsel and despised my every re-*

buke. Therefore they shall eat the fruit of their own way, and be filled to the full with their own fancies. For the turning away of the simple will slay them, and the complacency of fools will destroy them; But whoever listens to me will dwell safely, and will be secure, without fear of evil.

What is the relationship between knowledge and vision? Knowledge is the fuel for vision. Fuel is an energy source. Fuel is something consumed to produce something else. You consume knowledge to produce vision. Knowledge is the energy to fulfill your vision. You must know how to do things before you can accomplish them.

Knowledge produces the vision that directs your steps and determines your daily goals.

What you do today will determine what you get tomorrow. If you do nothing today, you will get nothing tomorrow. The Kingdom of Heaven is built upon the principle of sowing and reaping. We plant today for tomorrow's harvest. Your vision is validated and confirmed by your actions today!

Knowledge is the protectorate of vision.

Not only does knowledge fuel the vision, but it also protects the vision. "Protectorate" means a relationship of protection and partial control. The knowledge you learn and possess will be used to protect and control your vision.

A lack of either vision or knowledge leads to destruction. However, the combination of the two produce a vision that is validated by your actions and brings the necessary resources to make it happen

Some have vision, but no knowledge; others have knowledge with no vision. Success comes when the two are joined together. Noted Physicist, Albert Szent-Gyorgi once said, "A discovery is said to be an accident meeting a prepared mind." Knowledge prepares our mind for discovery and brings focus to vision.

PERSONAL REFLECTIONS

Chapter Two
Write the Vision

1. Habakkuk 2:2 states to write the vision and make it plain. What is the vision that you have for your life?

2. The Law of Entropy states that a system left unattended will go from order to chaos. Describe a situation in your life where this has happened to you.

3. Hosea 4:6 claims that people are destroyed for a lack of knowledge. Relate how you have seen this happen during your lifetime.

4. Proverbs 1:20 says that wisdom is crying out in the open squares or the market place. How can you access this wisdom?

5. Knowledge is the protectorate of vision. How does knowledge fuel and protect vision?

CHAPTER THREE

WHAT IS VISION?

Proverbs 29:18
Where there is no vision, the people perish.

Few succeed because they are destined; however, most succeed because they are determined. In other words, most succeed because of what they do in order to make things happen. The Word ensures our success in Joshua 1:8 which says, "This Book of the Law shall not depart from your mouth...observe to do according to all that is written in it. For then you will make your way prosperous, and then you will have good success." What are you doing to have success?

Your vision becomes what you are doing!

Visions are similar to dreams where supernatural insight or awareness is given by revelation. The difference between a dream and a vision is that dreams occur only during sleep, while visions can happen while a person is awake.

> *Daniel 10:7-9*
> *And I, Daniel, alone saw the vision, for the men who were with me did not see the vision; but a great terror fell upon them, so that they fled to hide themselves. Therefore I was left alone when I saw this great vision, and no strength remained in me; for my vigor was turned to frailty in me, and I retained no strength.*

Daniel had been praying for twenty-one days. On the twenty-first day of prayer, his eyes were opened to another dimension - the spiritual realm. There is a realm where spiritual beings exist, some of which are angels. Occasionally, people are allowed to see into the angelic world.

Sometimes this happens when people are awake and sometimes when they are asleep. Visions and dreams should be a regular part of our

Christian life. Daniel had a vision into the spiritual realm and he immediately fell to his knees. We are told that a messenger angel was commissioned to go to Daniel on the first day of his prayer.

The answer was released on the first day that Daniel prayed.

However, the answer took twenty-one days to reach him. You may feel like you have prayed and prayed, but your prayer is falling on deaf ears. Be encouraged when you pray in faith, God heard you from the first day. The enemy wants to delay your answer long enough to allow discouragement and depression to overtake you.

After praying and having done all to stand, then stand strong; knowing that your Father has sent your answer. The angel was sent forth immediately with the answer, but encountered some resistance along the way.

> *Daniel 10:11-14*
> *And he said to me, "O Daniel, man greatly beloved, understand the words that I speak to you, and stand upright, for I have now been sent to you." While he was speaking this word to me, I stood trembling. Then he said to me, "Do not fear, Daniel, for from the first day*

that you set your heart to understand, and to humble yourself before your God, your words were heard; and I have come because of your words. But the prince of the kingdom of Persia withstood me twenty-one days; and behold, Michael, one of the chief princes, came to help me, for I had been left alone there with the kings of Persia. Now I have come to make you understand what will happen to your people in the latter days, for the vision refers to many days yet to come."

The angel revealed future events to Daniel and said these events were already recorded in the Scripture of Truth.

The hallways of Heaven are currently displaying your future and destiny to all!

What validated Daniel's vision of the future? The answer to that question is found in what Daniel did from that day forward. The vision became the map for his daily steps. Those future events that were revealed became the key to what Daniel did in his everyday life!

Some think visions are full of glory and excitement. However, not all visions are full of grandeur. Visions often require hard work to be accomplished. The Lord wants us to cooperate with His vision for us and do what we can to fulfill it. We do our part and God will do His. Many visions that are given to prophets, speak of events that are not always grand and glorious.

> *Daniel 10:15-19*
> *When he had spoken such words to me, I turned my face toward the ground and became speechless. And suddenly, one having the likeness of the sons of men touched my lips; then I opened my mouth and spoke, saying to him who stood before me, "My lord, because of the vision my sorrows have overwhelmed me, and I have retained no strength. For how can this servant of my lord talk with you, my lord? As for me, no strength remains in me now, nor is any breath left in me."*

The vision that Daniel was given did not produce a grand and glorious feeling. It produced a feeling of sorrow so overwhelming that all of his strength faded and even his breath left him. You may feel that your world is full of sorrows to the point of being overwhelmed beyond your ability to recover. However, God does not leave us in this position of failure. He always provides a way and means to turn things around and give us strength. He always makes a way of escape and His way always leads to success.

> *Daniel 18:19*
> *Then again, the one having the likeness of a man touched me and strengthened me. And he said, "O man greatly beloved, fear not! Peace be to you; be strong, yes, be strong!" So when he spoke to me I was strengthened, and said, "Let my lord speak, for you have strengthened me."*

When the angel spoke, Daniel was strengthened!

Sometimes all we need to hear is the voice of the Lord in our spirit and strength will come. Knowing that God hears and cares is enough to bring joy into our lives and into our situation. Jeremiah 8:10 says that the joy of the Lord is our strength. Happiness is a product of our mind, but joy is a product of our spirit.

Joy is produced when our human spirit is in contact with our Heavenly Father about our life and situation. In Daniel's case, the angel spoke and Daniel was strengthened. God always knows what you need and how you need it! God released a vision to Daniel of the future of his people and his country.

Daniel was greatly concerned about his country and his people. Their previous kings led the people away from God and into sin. Concerning the destiny of a nation, it is critical to have godly leaders with the ability to hear the voice of the Lord! The Kings of Judah wandered away from God and followed their own purpose rather than the purpose God had for them.

As sin abounded, Judah's time as a sovereign nation came to an end. The Babylonians captured them, destroyed their cities and made them slaves. Daniel, himself, was a slave at this time. His situation was desperate; his need was great. Was Daniel and his people about to be removed from the face of the earth because of their sin? His desperation drove Daniel to pray and God answered him with visions and angelic visitations.

The purpose of these visions was two-fold: to give guidance and direction to God's servant in that day and also to foretell the future of Judah and their captors.

One of Daniel's visions, for example, told of the future coming of the Messiah.

> *Daniel 8:15-20*
> *Then it happened, when I, Daniel, had seen the vision and was seeking the meaning, that suddenly there stood before me one having*

> *the appearance of a man. And I heard a man's voice between the banks of the Ulai, who called, and said, "Gabriel, make this man understand the vision." So he came near where I stood, and when he came I was afraid and fell on my face; but he said to me, "Understand, son of man, that the vision refers to the time of the end." Now, as he was speaking with me, I was in a deep sleep with my face to the ground; but he touched me, and stood me upright. And he said, "Look, I am making known to you what shall happen in the latter time of the indignation; for at the appointed time the end shall be."*

Many times we focus on the future tense of the vision and forget about the guidance and direction it gives for today. Daniel was given a future vision of the Messiah to guide and direct his steps for every day living. What validated Daniel's future vision? His actions from that day forward validated his vision.

Daniel had been granted special access to see the future in order to guide his present-day steps. What you see in your future should guide the decisions and steps you make today!

The path to your future begins with the steps for today.

If your vision is to share a testimony or revelation in a book, then you have to start writing it today. The word *"vision"* can be defined as the faculty of sight; eyesight; something that is or has been seen.

The word *"vision"* means to see. What you SEE produces the steps that you take! If you are walking down the road, you have to see where the road is taking you. If you want to cross a street, you need to see if the street is safe to cross. If you were in the middle of a busy intersection and chose not to believe that the cars speeding past would hit you, the reality of the situation would "crash" into you quickly.

Your vision is designed to take you into your future, but it is also the means that you use to SEE the steps that you need to take today.

> *Acts 16:9-10*
> *And a vision appeared to Paul in the night; There stood a man of Macedonia and prayed him, saying, Come over into Macedonia, and help us. And after he had seen the vision, immediately we endeavoured to go into Macedonia, assuredly gathering that the Lord*

had called us for to preach the gospel unto them. (KJV)

Most historians claim the author of the book of Acts was Luke, the physician and the traveling companion of Paul and author of Luke's Gospel. This vision became known as the Macedonian Call which brought the Gospel to Europe and the Americas. Today, we are the fruit of this vision and call!

Your vision does not die with you, but continually produces fruit long after you are gone.

Paul received the vision and immediately made plans to leave. How did Paul have the finances to leave one continent and go to another? Do you know why God does not speak to most people like this? He does not often speak like this in today's world because most people cannot "up and go" anywhere or anytime.

Most people have this commitment and that commitment or this bill and that bill. It takes 4-6 weeks just to get a passport to go to another country. God cannot speak urgently to most people because they are not ready to go. It seems reasonable that every believer should have a passport in hand and money in the bank to go at a moment's notice... but we have our boats, and our cars, and our homes...

The late Pastor John Osteen once said, "Rather than make a living, make a life."

Acts 16:10 says that Paul made plans immediately to go. What validated his vision? Paul's actions validated his vision; he was ready to go. Remember that a God-given vision carries with it the resources and the finances to carry it and to carry you. Noted pastor and worship leader, Robert Gay says, "What God orders, He pays for." This is called pro-vision. Provision means to provide *"what is needed"* to produce the vision and comes from two words: produce and vision. Paul was prepared and provision was there to meet him.

Success comes when preparation meets opportunity.

Minister and author Ralph Waldo Emerson said, "People only see what they are prepared to see." We must educate and prepare ourselves to see what God has for us. The word *"vision"* is derived from the Hebrew meaning to "perceive." It is defined as a supernatural presentation to the spirit or mind of a person while awake.

Vision is what you SEE and is validated by what you DO! As you begin to do that for which you were created, your purpose becomes revealed. Your purpose is not hidden from you; it is hidden for you. God has placed hidden talents and abilities on the inside of you that He is waiting to reveal.

As you begin to see and do, your vision focuses and your purpose rises. Keys to your purpose can be found in your daily routine. Where are you spending your time? What are the things you enjoy doing on a regular basis? According to pastor and teacher Mike Murdock, the things that make you angry or the things that make you cry are indicators to why you are on this planet.

Vision makes you who you are. Vision equips you to perform. Vision becomes your beacon of light directing your life. Vision controls your speech and controls your friendships. Vision controls your thoughts and your decisions. Vision establishes your character. Vision produces your commitment and vision always includes others.

The real you is waiting to be discovered.

PERSONAL REFLECTIONS

Chapter Three
What is Vision?

1. Proverbs 29:18 claims that where there is no vision, the people perish. What does this mean to you?

2. Joshua 1:8 provides the steps to guarantee success. How can you use this in your life today?

3. The path to your future begins with the steps that you take today. What steps can you use to get to your vision?

4. Success comes when preparation meets opportunity. What opportunities are looking for you and how can you be prepared when they show up?

5. The real you is waiting to be discovered. What will that person look like when he or she shows up?

CHAPTER FOUR

PASSION AND PURPOSE

Exodus 9:16
Indeed for this purpose I have raised you up, that I may show My power in you, and that My name may be declared in all the earth.

God has placed within each person a vision that is designed to give purpose and meaning to your life. The essence of VISION is to see farther than your physical eyes can look. Vision is not just to see what is, but also to see what can be and make it a reality

Vision is the key to fulfilling your life's purpose.

One of the greatest gifts that God has given humanity is not sight, but vision. Sight is a function of the eyes, but vision is a function of the heart. When you have no vision, you will simply relive the past with disappointments and failures.

However, as long as you have vision - the ability to see beyond the present circumstances - you can move towards your purpose and declare it a REALITY. God has given every person a vision for their life, as well as one or more giftings which enable the fulfillment of that vision.

Paul said in Romans 12:6, "Having then gifts differing according to the grace that is given to us." We have been given a grace and gifts to fulfill our God-given vision. Often people do things because they HAVE to do them. However, VISION enables you to do things because you have DECIDED to cooperate with God's plan and accomplish it according to your purpose.

The plans and purposes for your life are hidden inside your desires and wants.

Psalms 37:3-5
Trust in the LORD, and do good;
Dwell in the land, and feed on His
faithfulness. Delight yourself also

in the LORD, And He shall give you the desires of your heart. Commit your way to the LORD, Trust also in Him, And He shall bring it to pass.

In Psalms 37, there are three main keys to releasing God's purpose in your life: trusting, delighting, and committing. As you focus on God, He focuses on you! We again see the Kingdom principle of sowing and reaping at work. As you sow focus, you will reap focus. When you delight yourself in the Lord, He will GIVE YOU or place inside of you the desires of your heart.

The literal translation of this passage is: *Delight yourself in the Lord and He will reveal the plan and purpose for your life.* As you read and delight yourself in God's Word, your purpose is revealed. Even our Lord Jesus went to God's Word to reveal His purpose.

Luke 4:16-21
So He came to Nazareth, where He had been brought up. And as His custom was, He went into the synagogue on the Sabbath day, and stood up to read. And He was handed the book of the prophet Isaiah. And when He had opened the book, He found the place where it was written: "The Spirit

> *of the LORD is upon Me, Because He has anointed Me To preach the gospel to the poor; He has sent Me to heal the brokenhearted, To proclaim liberty to the captives And recovery of sight to the blind, To set at liberty those who are oppressed; To proclaim the acceptable year of the LORD." Then He closed the book, and gave it back to the attendant and sat down. And the eyes of all who were in the synagogue were fixed on Him. And He began to say to them, "Today this Scripture is fulfilled in your hearing."*

Jesus goes into a synagogue and turns the scroll to a specific set of verses and begins to read, "the Spirit of the Lord is upon Me". If Jesus needed to go to the Scriptures to reveal His purpose, we do, too.

It is incredibly easy to get caught up in an "activity trap" and the "busy-ness" of life. We can spend our lives working hard at climbing the ladder of success only to discover that it is leaning against the wrong wall! It is possible to be busy in life and not be effective.

Passion is where you spend your time.

Your passion has become where you are spending your time. Look at your life and take stock of what you are doing and where you are spending your time. Is it in God's Word? Is it with your family? Your purpose is hidden in those daily activities.

You cannot fail with a God-activated purpose.

Proverbs 16:3
Commit to the LORD whatever you do, and your plans will succeed. (NIV)

God has a plan for your success, not your failure. God cannot give you failure because He does not have any failure in Him. He only knows success.

What would you do if you knew you could not fail?

God has created everyone with a personal purpose. The enemy may say that your life is the result of chance and the decisions you make are unimportant.

Ephesians 2:10
For we are God's workmanship, created in Christ Jesus to do good works, which God prepared in advance for us to do.

The Lord God has already prepared in advance the good works that He has planned for you. Those works are already recorded and on display in the hallways of Heaven.

> *Jeremiah 29:11-14*
> *For I know the plans I have for you," declares the LORD, "plans to prosper you and not to harm you, plans to give you hope and a future. Then you will call upon me and come and pray to me, and I will listen to you. You will seek me and find me when you seek me with all your heart (NIV).*

God knows the plans He has for you! It is God's plan for you to have hope and a future. The enemy will try to steal, kill and destroy your hopes and dreams, but God has a plan for your life that will not harm you.

Unfortunately, the lack of purpose and unfulfilled potential is epidemic in our world. For most people, their lives do not reflect who they truly are or what they can become. Too many voices are silent. Too many books are unwritten. Too many songs are unsung.

Now is the time and this is the season for change.

It has been said that the definition of insanity is doing the same thing over and over, but expecting different results. It is time to do something different. What you are living now is not a dress-rehearsal for your future. Today, God is encouraging His people to step up to the plate.

God is your batting coach and the ball has already been thrown. It is time for you to swing the bat and knock the enemy out of the park. Now is the time to find your voice and release His Word into the earth!

PERSONAL REFLECTIONS

Chapter Four
Passion and Purpose

1. Vision is the key to fulfilling your life's purpose. What purpose does God have for your life?

2. The plan and purpose that God has for your life is hidden inside your wants and desires. What are the things you want to accomplish in your life?

3. What would you do if you knew you could not fail?

4. What would you do if you did not have to work for money?

5. Now is the time and this is the season for change. Describe the things that you would like to change in your life.

CHAPTER FIVE

DISCOVERY TIME

Matthew 6:33
But seek first the kingdom of God and His righteousness, and all these things shall be added to you.

Discovery is often a challenging journey. However, the journey is easy when you know the way. Once Christopher Columbus discovered the new world, it became easy for others to follow. There is a story about Columbus after he discovered the new world:

Columbus was invited to a banquet in his honor for discovering the New World. One guest was jealous of the attention Columbus was getting and began to ridicule him and claim that anyone could have found the New World. The guest then glares at Columbus for a reply.

Instead of replying and getting snared in a trap, Columbus asks all the guests to make an egg stand on one end. All try but no one can; the egg keeps falling over. The jealous guest then claims that it cannot be done and glares at Columbus again. Columbus then takes an egg and gently taps it on the table, denting one end and leaves it standing. The jealous guest exclaims that anyone could do it that way. Columbus replies, yes, now that you know how. Once I found the way to the New World, anyone can follow it there.

The key to discovery is to see things differently from everyone else. Dr. Albert Szent-Gyorgyi (1893-1986) a noted Hungarian-U.S. biochemist once said: "Discovery consists of seeing what everybody has seen, and thinking what nobody has thought."

We call this "thinking outside the box" or "boldly going where no man has gone before." Columbus did not focus on just being status quo or using the maps that everyone else was using; he chose to use a new map and new compass. He dared to meet the edge of the world and risk falling off.

The real reason that Columbus believed the unbelievable - reaching the New World and not falling off the end of the Earth - was because God gave him a verse out of Proverbs.

> *Proverbs 8:27*
> *When he prepared the heavens, I was there: when he set a compass upon the face of the depth: (KJV)*

Every sailor knew that a compass was round. The New King James Version translates this Scripture as, "He drew a circle upon the face of the deep." The earth was round. Columbus chose to be grounded and rooted in the Word of God, not the current wisdom of men.

Historians have tried to silence the voice of truth. Most school children are no longer taught that Columbus was a Christian or that he had a vision from God. The Lord was directing him to be a "Christ-bearer" to a New World, which is what his name means.

Columbus dared to follow his destiny. Today, we know what Columbus thought and believed because he wrote it down! He assembled a collection of Scriptures in a work entitled, ***Libro de las Profecias*** (translated as ***Book of Prophecies***) and shared the belief in his destiny to discover the "isles of the sea" as mentioned in Isaiah 24:15. Columbus believed in his destiny and was willing to seek the Lord for a way to discover it.

The truth about Columbus does not come out in school books or even our library reference works. There is a war going on in our society today and that war is to silence the Christian voice. Progressive Secularists and Modernists have tried to silence the Christian voices of the past. Now, they are trying to silence the Christian voices of today.

It is time to silence the enemy by releasing our voice today!

If Columbus had not written a book about his beliefs and journeys, then the real truth of his life and mission would be lost forever. It is critical today for believers to record dreams, prophecies, visions and revelations in a book.

Because Columbus wrote it down in a book, he speaks the truth to us today.

Columbus not only used a physical compass to find his destiny but his greatest tool was using his moral compass and setting the Word of God as his standard or his "true north" setting.

A compass is only as good as its "true north" setting. There are factors that affect the "true north setting" of a real compass. Physical factors such as the curvature of the earth and magnetic properties all affect true north.

The same is true for our Moral Compass. Our true north setting is affected by the curvature of our life to the Word of God and our magnetism towards the Bible.

The path to your destiny is only as good as your true north setting!

A change in one degree of a ship sailing from New York and heading east will determine if that ship arrives in England or Spain. These are two very different destinations. Without a proper true north setting, you may even end up in Africa and miss Europe altogether.

People trapped in adultery, addiction, or any sin may wake up one day and wonder how they arrived at that destination. However, when you look back at their lives, you can track a degree change here and another one there. You might see scenes of a little flirting at work or a little drink on the way home from work. A degree of change here and there off your true north setting will take you to the wrong destiny.

We are required to check our true north setting and make the correct adjustments on the course of our life to ensure that we arrive at the right destination. This is why it is absolutely vital for every believer to be committed to the Word of God and planted in a local church. Without that pastoral oversight of our souls, we will likely drift off course.

> *Psalms 92:13*
> *Those who are planted in the house of the LORD Shall flourish in the courts of our God.*

Noted Psalmist and author Pastor Robert Gay has recorded a tremendous revelation in his book entitled ***Planted*** about the need that we have as believers to be planted in a local church. Only those that are planted in the house of the Lord will flourish in the plan and purpose prepared for them by God. Too many people try to follow their own paths and end up in a different place than what God intended.

Sometimes we get focused on the wrong thing. Again, let us look at the law of entropy - a system left to itself will tend towards disorder.

Activity is not always the answer either. Many times people spend time and energy climbing up the ladder of success only to find out that the ladder is against the wrong wall!

> *Proverbs 14:12*
> *There is a way that seems right*

to a man, but its end is the way of death.

This scripture is so important that it is repeated twice in the Bible; it is found also in Proverbs 16:25. God is emphasizing that many times we head off on the journey of discovery only to get side-tracked and veer off course.

It all started with a degree of change here and a degree of change there. Magnetic north looks a lot like true north; you can even find it on your compass. However, if you followed magnetic north instead of true north, the culmination of your journey could differ a great deal depending on where you are in the world.

Real discovery begins when we get alone with God and listen to Him.

If you did not have to "work" to generate income, what would you do?

When Elijah was quiet and alone with God, the Lord spoke about Elijah's purpose:

1 Kings 19:11-12
Then He said, "Go out, and stand on the mountain before the LORD." And behold, the LORD passed by, and a great and strong wind tore into the mountains and broke the

> *rocks in pieces before the LORD, but the LORD was not in the wind; and after the wind an earthquake, but the LORD was not in the earthquake; and after the earthquake a fire, but the LORD was not in the fire; and after the fire a still small voice.*

The voice of the Lord was not in the strong wind, the fire or the earthquake. Elijah discovered the voice of the Lord for his life as a still small voice quietly and confidently calling to him and guiding him.

> *1 Kings 19:9-10*
> *And there he went into a cave, and spent the night in that place; and behold, the word of the LORD came to him, and He said to him, "What are you doing here, Elijah?" So he said, "I have been very zealous for the LORD God of hosts; for the children of Israel have forsaken Your covenant, torn down Your altars, and killed Your prophets with the sword. I alone am left; and they seek to take my life."*

Have you ever been in this place of feeling alone and rejected? Are you there now? If so, then I have encouragement for you. The same

God that found Elijah in the cave feeling alone and rejected is the same God that knows where you are today. He knows what you are going through and He has the answer.

"When you are going through hell, don't stop!"

The great psalmist and Ambassador of Praise, Dr. Ron Kenoly, recorded a song once that said, "When you're going through hell, don't stop. Go ahead, go ahead, go ahead, go ahead, don't stop."

The word of the Lord for you today is "Don't Stop!" Keep on going. Even Elijah wanted to quit because he felt like he was the only one left. However, God did not leave Elijah in the predicament or the place in which he was found. The Lord will not leave you there either!

> *1 Kings 19:13*
> *So it was, when Elijah heard it, that he wrapped his face in his mantle and went out and stood in the entrance of the cave. Suddenly a voice came to him, and said, "What are you doing here, Elijah?"*

The voice of the Lord came to Elijah in the cave. When he heard it, he wrapped himself in his mantle. His mantle represented his gifting from God. When he wrapped himself in his gift, God began to restore him.

God told him to anoint two kings and anoint Elisha as his replacement. Scripture records that he only anointed Elisha. Elisha had to finish his task of anointing the two kings. Yet, the anointing had to happen. The declaration that God made to Elijah was as real as the cave that Elijah was hiding in. Even though Elijah did not complete this task, the task had to be completed.

Elisha not only picked up the mantle of Elijah, but he is required to complete the tasking that God gave earlier to Elijah. The declarations which God made to Elijah were recorded in the hallways of Heaven and they had to be fulfilled. There is an important principle at work in these passages.

The anointing stays in the earth.

PERSONAL REFLECTIONS

Chapter Five
Discovery Time

1. Matthew 6:33 says to seek first the Kingdom of God and all these things will be added to you. How can you apply this Scripture to your life?

2. The key to discovery is to see things differently from everyone else. What keys can you use in your life to discover your purpose?

3. The path to your destiny is only as good as your true north setting. What factors can influence your true north setting?

4. Psalm 92:13 states that those who are planted in the house of the Lord will flourish in the courts of God. How does becoming a part of a local church affect your future?

5. Trials and tribulations are a part of every person's life. What do you do when the storms of life come your way?

CHAPTER SIX

THE ANOINTING STAYS IN THE EARTH

1 John 2:27
But the anointing which you have received from Him abides in you, and you do not need that anyone teach you; but as the same anointing teaches you concerning all things, and is true, and is not a lie, and just as it has taught you, you will abide in Him.

The anointing abides in you. When you write and publish what God reveals to you, the anointing will abide in the Earth. We have the revelation and understanding of Elijah and Elisha because it was written down!

My good friend and mentor, Bishop Gerald Doggett, teaches that the anointing that was in Elijah was transferred to Elisha. However, Elisha did not have anyone to transfer the anointing to until years after his death. When men threw a dead man into the pit with Elisha's bones, the man sprang to life and carried Elisha's anointing away with him.

> *2 Kings 13:21*
> *So it was, as they were burying a man, that suddenly they spied a band of raiders; and they put the man in the tomb of Elisha; and when the man was let down and touched the bones of Elisha, he revived and stood on his feet.*

The anointing stays in the earth and its purpose is to bless future generations. The anointing is an energy. Science teaches that energy cannot be created or destroyed but it is transferred from one form to another. This process is called the Law of the Conservation of Energy.

The anointing cannot be created or destroyed, but it can be transferred from one to another.

All anointing comes from God and it is His alone. Many times people come to believe that the anointing belongs to them and it is there for their own personal use and enjoyment. Those people are deceived. The anointing does not belong to any man. It comes from God to enable us to do His good pleasure and to accomplish His plan and purpose for our life on this earth.

You must find your voice and release it into this earth for future generations. If you will release it, then it will stay! If you will write it, then all generations will have access to the anointing and truth that God has entrusted to you.

This may sound foreign to you. However, God's thoughts and our thoughts are not always the same.

> *Isaiah 55:8-9*
> *"For My thoughts are not your thoughts, Nor are your ways My ways," says the LORD. "For as the heavens are higher than the earth, So are My ways higher than your ways, And My thoughts than your thoughts."*

Discovery time with God allows us to utilize our moral compass and ensures that our true north setting is accurate. It keeps our thoughts in line with His thoughts. When navigating the wilderness of the changing times, a map is of limited worth. You must have a moral compass.

Whatever lies at the center of our lives becomes the primary source of our life support system. It has been said that you cannot talk your way out of problems into which you behaved yourself.

A renewed moral compass will always point to the right direction.

Many people seem to think that success in one area can compensate for failure in other areas of life. This is not true; a true north standard is required to reach the right location in life. The end DOES NOT justify the means.

In addition, time does not correct all things. Sometimes the Potter has to make a new vessel; especially when the old vessel has too many cracks and flaws. Time does not fix all things.

There is a difference between time and the compass. Time represents our commitments, appointments, schedules, goals, activities. It governs what we do with and how we manage our time.

The compass represents our vision, values,

principles, mission, conscience and direction. This indicates what we feel is important and how we lead our lives.

Our struggle comes when we sense a gap between time and the compass; when our actions do not contribute to what is truly important in our lives.

We have become masters of time management systems with PDAs, calendars and time management programs only to find that our location and destination have changed because along the way we lost our true north setting.

Is your ladder against the right wall?

We painstakingly climb the ladder of success rung by rung – the diplomas, the late nights, the promotions, and the time away from home - only to discover as we reach the top rung that the ladder is against the wrong wall. In our race to climb the ladder, we possibly neglect family, spouses and children; we do not always take the time to do what matters most.

The ladder is against the wrong wall. Yet we are unable to see it. We are too busy climbing to see that it is against the wrong wall; we do not realize that our true north setting has changed.

Mark 8:36
For what will it profit a man if he gains the whole world, and loses his own soul?

Why could we not see the ladder was against the wrong wall? If we are unable to see, then we have become blind in an area. We are unable to see because we have NO VISION. Vision allows us to be able to see the present.

Proverbs 29:18
Where there is no vision, the people perish: but he that keepeth the law, happy is he. (KJV)

Why are these people happy? When you understand and follow the principles of God and allow your inner man to follow that inner compass, you will find yourself at the top of the ladder against the right wall!

Having no vision is deadly, but there are also problems with division. Di-Vision means two visions; double vision produces double-mindedness.

James 1:8
A double minded man is unstable in all his ways. (KJV)

Instability is a result of being double-minded. We must eliminate di-vision in our hearts and minds. How do we deal with double-mindedness?

> *James 4:8*
> *Draw near to God and He will draw near to you. Cleanse your hands, you sinners; and purify your hearts, you double-minded.*

By purifying your heart, you can truly be set free from being double-minded. You must search your heart to see what is really important. Once discovered, you must ask if it lines up to the Word of God. What is really important to you? These answers will help you realize what is inside your heart.

For example, how many people on their deathbed wish they had spent more time at the office? None. People on their deathbed are more likely to wish they had spent more time with friends and family. It is sad that it sometimes takes death to help us realize what is really important in life. There is a better way and a better time to learn this valuable lesson.

Our moral compass reminds and prompts us to prioritize the most important things in our life. First, we need to plan our time with family and friends, then fill in the remainder of the schedule.

> *Proverbs 4:20-27*
> *My son, give attention to my words; Incline your ear to my sayings. Do not let them depart from your eyes; Keep them in the midst of your heart; For they are life to those who find them, and health to all their flesh. Keep your heart with all diligence, for out of it spring the issues of life. Put away from you a deceitful mouth, and put perverse lips far from you. Let your eyes look straight ahead, and your eyelids look right before you. Ponder the path of your feet, and let all your ways be established. Do not turn to the right or the left; Remove your foot from evil.*

Our moral compass serves as the guide for our heart. When we keep the moral compass set to true north, our compass is able to direct us into the future God has for us.

You cannot walk backwards into the future.

People who finish the race are those who base their life on the correct true north standard which is the Word of God. These people are drawn magnetically to the Bible and not to man's opinions, current fads or how the winds are blowing. It is this dependency upon the curvature of our life to the Word of God that will keep us on track!

If you were to pause and think seriously about the three or four most important things in your life, what would they be? Are they written down? Does your family know what they are? Can your spouse name them?

Are these important things receiving the care, emphasis and time that they deserve? We need to periodically review our true north setting standards and mark our progress towards these destinations. You might only need to adjust a degree or two or maybe even a 180 degree change. You can change that heading after you have made the proper adjustment towards the true north standard of God's Word.

Years ago I heard the late Pastor John Osteen repeat a strong confession about the Word. Now, I have taken his confession and made it my own. This daily confession will help keep your true north standard set to the Bible:

> *This is my Bible. It is the Word of God and it is God's Word to me today and everyday. I will read it. I will follow it. I will obey it. It is my "true north setting" and I will follow its direction to find my destiny. In Jesus' Name!*

Proverbs 4:20-27, quoted earlier, teaches us that God's principles provide three crucial tools for developing and following our moral compass:

1) The Scriptures are a guide; they help us stay on the right path and keep our ladder against the right wall.
2) The Scriptures are a guard; they keep our hearts and bodies protected.
3) The Scriptures are a gauge; they enable us to evaluate where we are and to determine if our ladder is against the right wall.

Success in the business world teaches us to fill our schedules and PDAs first and give our family, church, and friends the time remaining.

God is NOT the God of leftovers!

Many times, all this scheduling will do is increase the gap between time and the compass. The moral compass teaches us to first schedule the most important things in our life. Arrange your planner first with regard to your relationship with the Lord, for your spouse, your children, your church and then schedule the balance of your week.

Prioritize those things that are most important.

As you learn to listen to your moral compass by prioritizing the most important things first, your purpose will be revealed. Your purpose is hidden in your daily routine. It will be revealed based on what you do! Daniel received a vision and then began to walk it out in his daily life.

Once you have discovered that purpose and plan for your life (your vision), you need to write it down so that all who come after you can read and run with it! Once you have published your vision and purpose, it will become activated in your life and in the lives of those around you. It is at this time that you begin to impact your world!

PERSONAL REFLECTIONS

Chapter Six
The Anointing Stays in the Earth

1. The anointing cannot be created or destroyed, but it can be transferred from one person to another. Has this type of transference every occurred in your life?

2. A renewed moral compass will always point in the right direction. What can you do to keep your moral compass pointing in the right direction?

3. Many people have their ladder of success against the wrong wall. How would you counsel a friend if this happened to them?

4. No one on their deathbed wishes for more time in the office. What are the most important things in your life today?

5. As believers, we need to prioritize our lives. Take your list from question 4 and prioritize the items that you will work on this week.

CHAPTER SEVEN

IMPACT YOUR WORLD

Luke 4:43
He said to them, "I must preach the kingdom of God to the other cities also, because for this purpose I have been sent."

Jesus discovered his purpose from the Scriptures. He also used the Scriptures to share His purpose with others.

Luke 4:16-20
So He came to Nazareth, where He had been brought up. And as His custom was, He went into the syn-

> *agogue on the Sabbath day, and stood up to read. And He was handed the book of the prophet Isaiah. And when He had opened the book, He found the place where it was written: "The Spirit of the LORD is upon Me, because He has anointed Me to preach the gospel to the poor; He has sent Me to heal the brokenhearted, to proclaim liberty to the captives and recovery of sight to the blind. To set at liberty those who are oppressed. To proclaim the acceptable year of the LORD." Then He closed the book, and gave it back to the attendant and sat down. And the eyes of all who were in the synagogue were fixed on Him.*

His purpose was revealed and activated to all who were present. From that point forward, Jesus went about doing good and healing all who were oppressed of the devil (Acts 10:38). Jesus impacted His world and the world around Him.

When purpose is revealed and activated in your life, an energy called "passion" will be produced.

Activated passion is a by-product of revealed purpose.

Many times we try to "stir up" passion by trying to get excited about something; but, this is backwards to the way it should go. Passion does not produce purpose. It is fine and good to get excited about the things of the Lord, but that has nothing to do with purpose and passion.

There is nothing wrong with excitement. However, do not confuse excitement with purpose. Just because you get excited about a football game does not mean that your purpose is to sit around and watch football all the time!

Passion is a product of purpose.

Passion is released once purpose has been revealed! The last week in the life of Jesus is called the Passion Week. It is not because the week was full of excitement for Him. As a matter of fact, it was the worst week of His life.

The Passion Week was a product of the revealed purpose of Jesus. His purpose was to take back what had been stolen in the Garden of Eden. Mankind was created by God and the Lord wanted us back. We had to be redeemed or bought back.

Once Jesus revealed His purpose to the world through the reading of Isaiah 61, passion was released. This passion helped Him complete

His task of preaching the Kingdom of God. Once His purpose was completed, He sealed the new covenant with His sinless blood at Calvary.

When the plan and purpose of Jesus' life was revealed, He went about influencing and impacting His world. We must follow His example. In John 5:19 Jesus said, "The Son can do nothing of Himself, but what He sees the Father do; for whatever He does, the Son also does in like manner." As Christians, we are to be followers of Jesus and do the things that He did.

When our purpose is revealed, we should go about the business of the Kingdom which calls us to impact our world.

The anointing and vision that God has given you is the message that you are to bring to your world! Just as the Madman of Gadera went about publishing what Jesus had done for him, we should go about publishing what God has done for us. It is time to write!

> *Psalms 45:1*
> *My heart is overflowing with a good theme; I recite my composition concerning the King; My tongue is the pen of a ready writer.*

We must say it and we must write it. We must tell the world here and now; then, we must write it to equip future generations. God is raising up an army of warriors for this generation. Their assignment is not only to preach the Good News now, but write it for all generations to come.

To influence our world we need to become good communicators. Communication is not always giving orders and issuing commands for others to follow. There is an old story which shows the importance of proper communication:

A ship was sailing along one very dark and foggy night. The seaman on duty brought to the Captain's attention that a light was bearing straight ahead and was not moving despite sending a warning to change paths to avoid a collision. The Captain then sent the next message: "This is Captain I.M. Tough and I command you to move aside; we are coming through." The response came back immediately, "This is Seaman Sam Smith, you need to turn aside at once." The Captain became furious. He radioed to headquarters asking for information on any ship in his area. The response came back that there were no ships in his area. The Captain, believing this ship to be a small wayward vessel responds back to the unmoving light, "This is the unsinkable Battleship Ironside, turn aside immediately or risk certain destruction." The response came back once again,

"This is the lighthouse on the rocks, you turn aside immediately or risk certain destruction."

Communication must be a two-way street or we may end up on the rocks! The key to effective communication is not in speaking, but in listening.

Communication begins when we seek first to understand what the other person is saying. How many times have you been in a conversation where you are waiting to speak your point rather than focusing on what the other person is saying?

Communication begins when we LISTEN, rather than SPEAK.

When communicating, how often do we have all the answers before we even hear of the problems? People have a tendency to rush in to fix things with their own good advice. However, we often fail to take the time to discover the real problem.

Are you listening with the intent to respond or with the intent to understand? How do you tell the difference?

While the other person is talking, are you formulating your answer and waiting until you can jump in with your solution? Do you listen and repeat back what is said and then think of your "advice" or comment?

Most listen with the intent to respond rather than the intent to understand.

According to noted author Dr. Stephen Covey, there are five levels of listening:

1. **Ignoring:** no effort.
2. **Pretend Listening**: the occasional grunt. Little to no eye contact.
3. **Selective Listening:** Hearing key words and responding immediately.
4. **Focused Listening:** Focusing on what is said and comparing it to your own experiences.
5. **Empathic Listening:** Identification with and understanding of another's situation, feelings, and motives.

To understand another person, we need to listen first and not speak. We often take our own thoughts and feelings and fill in the blanks of another person's life. **Empathic listening** is to see the world through the eyes of another to gain their understanding.

In order to influence and impact our world, communication is critical. However, before we can start communicating, we must first listen to our mentors and advisors since there is safety in a multitude of counselors. In addition and more importantly, we must also keep our focus on listening intently to what the Lord is saying. As we listen to the thoughts of God, we can know what is needed to impact and influence our world.

Once that information has been received from the Lord, we are required to pass it on. God does not give us revelation and information so we can sit around and think about how smart we have become. There is a requirement placed upon us to share that information.

Writing and publishing books are one of the most expedient means which God has given us to impact our world!

The greatest thoughts, revelations and insights in our generation come from people who spend time in the presence of the Lord. However, some have grown cold and no longer hunger and thirst for righteousness. We must continue to return to the well for a fresh drink.

It's time to get THAT back!

PERSONAL REFLECTIONS

Chapter Seven
Impact Your World

1. Jesus went to the Scriptures to find His purpose. Find and discuss three Scriptures that point to your purpose.

2. Passion is a product of purpose. What are you most passionate about?

3. To impact our world, we need to be effective communicators. What can you do to become a more effective communicator?

4. How can you tell the difference between listening with the intent to understand and the intent to respond?

5. Discuss the five levels of listening on page 69. What level do you primarily use?

CHAPTER EIGHT

I WANT THAT BACK

Matthew 18:11
For the Son of Man has come to save that which was lost.

Matthew records that Jesus came to save **THAT** which was lost - not **THEM** which were lost. In Christendom, we tend to go after them, but Jesus came to save **THAT** which was lost.

Today, the church is more inclined to get a lot of them, but not much of **THAT**. Whereas, the Scripture teaches if we can get **THAT**, He will bring them.

What was lost? Where was it lost?

To find out what was lost, we must go back to the beginning. In Genesis, we read:

> *Genesis 2:7-8*
> *And the LORD God formed man of the dust of the ground, and breathed into his nostrils the breath of life; and man became a living being. The LORD God planted a garden eastward in Eden, and there He put the man whom He had formed.*

God planted a garden eastward in Eden. The Hebrew word for "eastward" means the front of, the place, or the spot. The word "garden" comes from the Hebrew word which means to hedge about, to protect or defend.

"Eden" is a Hebrew word that means pleasure, delicate, or delight. The word "Eden" in the Hebrew language is composed of five jots and a tittle for a total of six strokes. Each stroke has a meaning: moment, spot, presence, pleasant, delightful atmosphere and open door.

Pastor and teacher, Dr. Myles Munroe, teaches that "Eden" literally means *"the spot for the moment where an open door takes you to the pleasant and delightful place of God's pres-*

ence." Eden is an atmosphere and an environment more than a physical place. Eden was the spot where mankind was when God came down to visit and receive worship.

Today's Eden is the presence of God at your spot!

> *Genesis 3:8*
> *And they heard the sound of the LORD God walking in the garden in the cool of the day, and Adam and his wife hid themselves from the presence of the LORD God among the trees of the garden.*

Adam and his wife heard the door to their "spot" open and knew God was coming to visit them to receive fellowship and worship. Because of sin, they hid themselves from His presence; they could no longer be in the spot with His presence. They lost **THAT**.

Adam and his wife lost the atmosphere and the environment to walk in God's presence.

Matthew 18:11 reads, "The Son of Man came to save **THAT** which was lost." Jesus came to redeem the spot for the moment, where an open door takes you to the pleasant and delightful place of God's presence.

Psalms 22:3
But thou art holy, O thou that inhabitest the praises of Israel. (KJV)

God inhabits or dwells in the praises of His people. As you begin to praise God, He hears you and turns toward you with His presence. He hears the door open and knows that someone wants to walk with Him. It gets God's attention when someone desires fellowship with Him.

Your praise opens the door and God's response is to move towards you and release worship. The result is that mankind is once again in the spot for the moment where an open door takes you to the pleasant and delightful place of God's presence. Through your Christian experience, Eden has returned to Earth.

We need the presence of God!

Your natural environment is to be in the presence of God. It is unnatural to be anywhere else. Dr. Myles Munroe puts it best when he says, "We do not want the presence of God; we **need** the presence of God."

Just like a fish does not want water to survive, it needs it. It is unnatural for a fish to be out of water. To live and flourish, the fish must live in the right environment. If a fish is not in the right environment, it will flop and twist and do anything it can to return to its proper environment.

For mankind to live and flourish, we must be in the right environment which is the presence of God. This is why praise and worship is so crucial to the life of the church and the life of a believer. It creates the environment - the spot for the moment to be in God's presence.

The presence of God is so crucial that Jesus gave His life to save THAT which was lost.

As we enter into the presence of God, we commune with Him just as Adam did in the Garden of Eden. While we are in His presence, we can listen to what He has to say to today's generation.

This is exactly what happened to the Apostle John while he was on the Island of Patmos. He had been exiled there because the Romans had tried several times to kill him, but could not. A rumor began to circulate that John would never die.

After several unsuccessful attempts to kill him, the Romans banished him to the Island of Patmos. Their purpose was to keep him away from the people and shut him up! However, God had other plans.

> *Revelation 1:1-3*
> *The Revelation of Jesus Christ, which God gave Him to show His servants — things which must shortly take place. And He sent and signified it by His angel to His servant John, who bore witness to the word of God, and to the testimony of Jesus Christ, to all things that he saw. Blessed is he who reads and those who hear the words of this prophecy, and keep those things which are written in it; for the time is near.*

The Apostle John was given this tremendous revelation and prophecy not only for his time, but for all generations. Just think, if John had not written down this vision, it would be lost forever decaying in the grave along with countless other books not written.

> *Revelation 1:9-11*
> *I, John, both your brother and companion in the tribulation and kingdom and patience of Jesus Christ, was on the island that is called Patmos for the word of God and for the testimony of Jesus Christ. I was in*

> *the Spirit on the Lord's Day, and I heard behind me a loud voice, as of a trumpet, saying, "I am the Alpha and the Omega, the First and the Last," and, "What you see, write in a book and send it to the seven churches which are in Asia: to Ephesus, to Smyrna, to Pergamos, to Thyatira, to Sardis, to Philadelphia, and to Laodicea."*

John was in the spirit on the Lord's Day. Through his praise and worship, John opened that ancient door. The Lord God heard that familiar sound of someone opening the door into His presence and He responded with an eternal and life-giving vision.

While in the presence of the Lord, John was granted a vision and a prophecy for the seven churches in Asia. This prophecy applied not only to them, but also to us. John was further commanded to write down what he saw.

We must seek God's presence and take time to listen to Him. Obedience must always follow God's direction. The Apostle John had to be sent to Patmos in order for God to get him to write. In the same manner, God seemingly had the Apostle Paul jailed to write down the revelations he was given.

God gives us visions and prophecies so that we might see and write of the things present and the things to come. To share in the same blessings as the Apostles John and Paul, we must follow their examples.

We must return to the spot for the moment where the delightful presence of God awaits us. While we are in that spot, we should see and write for the edification of this generation as well as the generations to come!

Now is the time to make your pen as the pen of the "ready writer." Now is the time to fulfill the commission to publish abroad all that the Lord has done. Now is the time to be in the spot for the moment and record all that we see.

It is time to awaken the scribe within you.

PERSONAL REFLECTIONS

Chapter Eight
I Want that Back

1. Matthew 18:11 states that Jesus came to save that which was lost. What was lost and where was it lost?

2. What does the word "Eden" mean to you?

3. We need the presence of God in our daily life. How can we access the presence of God today?

4. How does praise and worship open the door for access to God's presence?

5. The Apostle John was given the book of Revelation in a vision while in exile on the Island of Patmos. How important is it to write down the things we get from God?

CHAPTER NINE

THE SCRIBE ANOINTING

Matthew 13:52
Then He said to them, "Therefore every scribe instructed concerning the kingdom of heaven is like a householder who brings out of his treasure things new and old."

The purpose of the scribe has been lost for many generations. What was once a highly respected position of trust and authority in the kingdom has been lost from the Kingdom of God. Additionally, the scribe anointing needs to be recovered for future generations.

The ancient Hebrew word for "scribe" is *caphar* and is pronounced "*saw-far.*" Therefore, a scribe was a person who "saw far" into the past and into the future for the good of the kingdom. This word first appears in the Bible in the book of Genesis.

> *Genesis 15:5*
> *And he brought him forth abroad, and said, Look now toward heaven, and tell the stars, if thou be able to number them: and he said unto him, So shall thy seed be. (KJV)*

One of the first promises to Abraham was the anointing of the *caphar*. This word is translated "to tell the number of" in the verse above. Abraham's seed was to be as the *caphar* or an innumerable amount of stars in the heavens. God is showing Abraham that his seed would extend far into the future and would be impossible to number.

Abraham and his seed are included in the *caphar* anointing

According to Galatians 3:29, believers are the seed of Abraham and in line to receive from the inheritance of Abraham.

> *Galatians 3:29*
> *And if you are Christ's, then you*

are Abraham's seed, and heirs according to the promise.

The *caphar* anointing that was promised to Abraham has been passed down to his seed. Since we are the spiritual heirs of Abraham, this anointing is available to believers. However, as with all blessings and promises of God, we must appropriate them and then release them into our lives. All of God's promises are "yes" and "amen" but we must activate them into our lives.

2 Corinthians 1:20
For all the promises of God in Him are Yes, and in Him Amen, to the glory of God through us.

The scribe anointing is available and ready for believers to activate.

The primary means of activating a scribe anointing is to write and publish the things that God has done in our lives. We are to tell of God's greatness and power. In Genesis 24:66, the word *caphar* is used to mean "to be told or to tell."

Genesis 24:66
And the servant told Isaac all things that he had done.

Throughout the first five books of the Bible, which is commonly called the Pentateuch and was written by Moses, *caphar* was translated "to number and to tell". However, in the Book of Judges, *caphar* undergoes another transformation.

> *Judges 5:14*
> *Out of Ephraim was there a root of them against Amalek; after thee, Benjamin, among thy people; out of Machir came down governors, and out of Zebulun they that handle the pen of the writer (KJV).*

The author of the Book of Judges is uncertain. However, the Jewish Talmud indicates that Samuel was the author. Regardless of the author, the word translated as "writer" is the word *caphar*. *Caphar* now includes the idea to number or to tell as well as to write.

The scribe anointing evolves to include those that handle the pen of the writer.

Moses wrote the first five books of the Bible and had obviously influenced the author of the Book of Joshua. However, the children of Israel found themselves in a position of not having anyone to tell and record about their existence.

How many cultures have come and gone because no one took the time to tell and record of their existence? God would not allow this to happen to His people Israel. The tribe of Zebulun was given the task of recording the exploits of God's chosen people.

Unfortunately, Judges six records that the children of Israel did evil in the sight of the Lord. Because of this, they were delivered into the hand of the Midianites for seven years. The tribe of Zebulun slowly began to record these events as well. The *caphar* anointing was expanded once again with the help of Gideon.

> *Judges 7:13-16*
> *And when Gideon had come, there was a man telling a dream to his companion. He said, "I have had a dream: To my surprise, a loaf of barley bread tumbled into the camp of Midian; it came to a tent and struck it so that it fell and overturned, and the tent collapsed." Then his companion answered and said, "This is nothing else but the sword of Gideon the son of Joash, a man of Israel! Into his hand God has delivered Midian and the whole camp." And so it was, when Gideon heard the telling of the dream and its interpretation,*

> *that he worshiped. He returned to the camp of Israel, and said, "Arise, for the LORD has delivered the camp of Midian into your hand."*

The *caphar* anointing was released in the telling of a dream.

Verse sixteen uses the word *caphar* in the telling of the dream. The *caphar* (telling) of the dream drove Gideon to his knees in worship. The scribe anointing will always drive us back to worship the One who provides the purpose for our life.

The tribe of Zebulun records the famous words for the Sword of the Lord and for Gideon from Judges 7:20 and further describes the route of the Midianites with Gideon's now famous 300 warriors. This *caphar* emboldened Gideon to strike against the Midianites and to deliver the children of Israel from their oppressors.

> *Judges 8:22-23*
> *Then the men of Israel said to Gideon, "Rule over us, both you and your son, and your grandson also; for you have delivered us from the hand of Midian." But Gideon said to them, "I will not rule over you, nor shall my son*

rule over you; the LORD shall rule over you."

Gideon understood that the key to success for the people of Israel was to rely upon the Lord God as their only king. Because of Gideon and his reliance upon the Lord, the land and the people were at peace for forty years until the time of his death.

Until the time of King David, the word *caphar* was used to number or to tell as well as to describe a dream. However, the word "scribe" had not been used. King David was the first person to tie the *caphar* to the word "scribe" as a prominent office in his Kingdom.

2 Samuel 8:17-18
Seraiah was the scribe... and David's sons were chief ministers.

King David not only elevated the description of the *caphar*, but the scribe was one of his most trusted advisors. Eventually, the scribe would become the second highest official in the king's court. King David also further expands the definition of the *caphar* and ties the scribe anointing to the spoken word as well as the written word.

Psalms 45:1
My heart is overflowing with a good theme; I recite my composi-

tion concerning the King; My tongue is the pen of a ready writer.

Psalms 45:1 pinnacles the path of the *caphar*. The scribe became the second most powerful person in the kingdom and David brought the purpose of the scribe back to the written word. The scribe continued through the ages and was even elevated to the position of priest as seen with the Prophet Ezra.

In Ezra 7:11, the Bible states that Ezra was a priest and a scribe. The scribe anointing has become the position that is responsible for keeping the Word of God for the people and also for its prophetic declaration.

It is in this prophetic declaration that the scribe anointing has reached its ultimate expression. The full expression of the scribe anointing can be found in the prophetic declaration of what God is saying.

Jeremiah 52:25 references the scribe as the person to bring the people together and instruct them. It was Jeremiah who had a personal scribe named Baruch that was charged with recording his prophecies.

Jeremiah 36:32
Then Jeremiah took another scroll and gave it to Baruch the scribe,

> *the son of Neriah, who wrote on it at the instruction of Jeremiah all the words of the book which Jehoiakim king of Judah had burned in the fire. And besides, there were added to them many similar words.*

Baruch was charged with recording the prophetic declarations of Jeremiah. Even though the King of Judah actually burned the book that contained Jeremiah's prophetic utterances, Baruch continued his writings of Jeremiah's prophecies.

The scribe anointing is housed in the prophetic word.

Even the king of the land could not hold back the prophetic word. God had released the scribe anointing in the earth which is where it would stay.

By the writing of the New Testament, the Scribe had become an office of influence and power throughout the land as Scribes and Pharisees ruled over the people. It was under this framework that Jesus spoke of the scribe. In Matthew 13:52, He said that every scribe which has been instructed about the Kingdom of Heaven is like a householder who brings out of his treasure things new and old.

The scribe became the person who held the keys to the Kingdom of Heaven. The owner of the house was the person with the keys. Those who have knowledge, revelation and understanding concerning the Kingdom are now required to bring out the treasure and share it.

Every person has a realm of influence. Every person has "their" world that needs to be impacted concerning the Kingdom. Every person has a voice that needs to be released to impact a world that groans and waits for the manifestation of the sons of God. The scribe anointing impacts the world for the Kingdom. It is time to awaken the scribe!

NOW IS THE TIME.

PERSONAL REFLECTIONS

Chapter Nine
The Scribe Anointing

1. Matthew 13:52 says that a scribe writes about things old and new. What are some things that you could write about?

2. Judges 7 tells us about the Word of the Lord coming to Gideon through the telling of a dream. What are some of the spiritual dreams that you have had?

3. Jeremiah 36:32 states that Jeremiah had a personal scribe to record his prophecies. What are some of the prophecies you have received?

4. Every person has a realm of influence. What are some of the areas that you have influence over?

5. What can you do to impact your world?

CHAPTER TEN

NOW IS THE TIME!

2 Corinthians 6:2
For He says: "In an acceptable time I have heard you, and in the day of salvation I have helped you." Behold, now is the accepted time.

Now is the time to find and release your words into your world. Once declared, your voice will remain in the earth for this generation and for all the generations to come.

However, the enemy Satan does not want you to release your words into this world. As you release your voice for God, the enemy's voice becomes diminished and has less influence.

When you release your voice and publish abroad all the things God has done, you discover that all the powers that are against Jesus Christ, become your enemy. Do not be afraid and do not back down. We cannot be caught unaware because we are at war with principalities and powers of darkness.

> *Ephesians 6:10-13*
> *Finally, my brethren, be strong in the Lord and in the power of His might. Put on the whole armor of God that you may be able to stand against the wiles of the devil. For we do not wrestle against flesh and blood, but against principalities, against powers, against the rulers of the darkness of this age, against spiritual hosts of wickedness in the heavenly places.*

As a soldier in the army of the Lord, we must learn to wrestle against principalities, rather than people. Every good soldier is first sent to boot camp. In God's BOOT CAMP, you are taught that God provides protective armor for the Christian soldier to win all the battles of life!

After becoming a Christian, you are NOT a volunteer in the Christian army.

You are not a volunteer in God's army, but you have been drafted and inducted as a soldier in the "family" business and business is good! Read what the spirit called Legion, which was in the madman from Gadera, had to say:

> *Luke 4:34*
> *Saying, Let us alone; what have we to do with thee, thou Jesus of Nazareth? art thou come to destroy us? I know thee who thou art; the Holy One of God.*

Knights of old put their armor on when they were ready for war. Demons tremble in the face of a true warrior. When you put on the armor of God and use the Name of Jesus, all that a demon can see is Jesus. According to James 2:19, we see that demons tremble at the sight of Jesus.

> *1 John 3:8*
> *He who sins is of the devil, for the devil has sinned from the beginning. For this purpose the Son of God was manifested, that He might destroy the works of the devil.*

Jesus came to destroy the works of the devil!

As Christians, we are at war with the enemy, Satan, and his cohorts. However, God has not left us defenseless in our battles. On the contrary, He has more than adequately equipped us to continue the mission of our Lord. In the same manner that Jesus was sent to destroy the works of the devil, we are sent also.

> *Ephesians 6:13-18*
> *Therefore take up the whole armor of God that you may be able to withstand in the evil day, and having done all, to stand. Stand therefore, having girded your waist with truth, having put on the breastplate of righteousness, and having shod your feet with the preparation of the gospel of peace; above all, taking the shield of faith with which you will be able to quench all the fiery darts of the wicked one. And take the helmet of salvation, and the sword of the Spirit, which is the word of God.*

After having done all we can do, we are to stand! The original Greek word for *stand* is "histemi" (his'-tay-mee). In various places, the King James Version of the Bible also translates the word *histemi* as: abide, appoint, bring, continue, covenant, establish, hold up, lay, present, set (up), stanch. *Histemi* properly denotes an upright and active position. It also means to set-up or establish. This is a military word with a military definition. "To setup and establish" an active position literally means to establish a military campaign or strategy.

As Christians, we sometimes do things backwards. We may try to put on the armor of God and then stand. Scripture says to setup and establish an active position or a military campaign and strategy, THEN put on the armor.

A Roman soldier puts his armor on to go to WAR. He did not put it on to create the plan of attack and then stand around and wait for the enemy to attack. A Roman soldier only understood one kind of war: PLAN AND ATTACK

The armor of God is not intended for a defensive encounter. The armor of God is put on when its time to go to WAR and DESTROY the works of the devil.

The victory has already been won by Jesus at Calvary. We are not just holding on to what we have and where we are; we are possessing our land. Set up and establish your campaign and having done all you can do to plan and prepare, put on your armor and attack the enemy.

Once we receive the master attack plan from the Lord, we are ready to suit up for war.

First, we must gird up or guard our waist with truth. The Word of God is truth. Knowledge of truth brings freedom. If you do not put the truth of God's Word around your waist, Satan, the father of all lies, will try to deceive you.

Next, we are to put on the breastplate of righteousness. This will protect our heart with right-standing when we receive our position in the Lord.

Then it is time to shod our feet with the preparation of the gospel of peace. Even in the midst of the battle, we may walk in the peace that passes understanding. We must walk in the benefits of our salvation; we must take this Good News out for all to hear.

The next step is to take the shield of faith with which you will be able to quench ALL the fiery darts of the wicked one. Faith in God will protect us from the enemy's onslaught of lies and deception.

With our body being armored and protected, it is time to take the helmet of salvation in order to renew and protect our mind. We are to be ever conscious of our place in God. As a Christian, we are told that we have the mind of Christ.

The first stage of battle always takes place in the mind.

Our weapon of choice for offense is the famous sword of the Spirit, which is the Word of God. The Greek word for *sword* is the word "machaira."

The Greeks were successful warriors who fought with a spear and defended with their shield. However, when the battle culminated in hand to hand combat, the *machaira* sword was the weapon of choice to bring fear to the enemy.

Machairas were effective and devastating weapons able to pierce a bronze helmet. The *machaira* was the single most feared weapon of the Greco-Roman Era. Many scholars believe that the *machaira* may have single-handedly pushed back the Persians in their attempts to conquer the Greeks.

The *machaira* was a two-edged, small yet lethal sword. This was the image that Paul was using when he wrote about the sword of the Spirit in Ephesians 6:18.

> *2 Corinthians 10:4*
> *For the weapons of our warfare are not carnal but mighty in God for pulling down strongholds.*

Our warfare is not against people, but against principalities, powers and rulers of darkness. The warfare is real and the weapons are real. However, the enemy is not a physical enemy and the weapons are not physical weapons.

Our weapons may not be physical weapons but they are powerful. The *machaira* sword that we use today is the "rhema" word or the spoken word of God

The *rhema* word is the revealed word or the spoken word.

God wants to reveal His plan and purpose to you in order that you may reveal it to others. However, you must have a plan to reveal His purpose!

Once you setup and establish your plan, you must clothe yourself in armor to go to war to release your voice and release the revealed word of the Lord.

Let us commit to obey the instructions given to the Apostle John as seen in the verse below. When we obey these words, the results will be powerful and eternal.

> *Revelation 1:19*
> *Write the things which you have seen, and the things which are, and the things which will take place after this.*

Once you have the voice of revelation to influence your world, then write it down and publish it abroad.

NOW IS THE TIME TO RELEASE YOUR WORDS!

PERSONAL REFLECTIONS

Chapter Ten
Now is the Time

1. What can you do to ensure that your voice will remain in the Earth for future generations?

2. 1 John 3:8 states that Jesus came to destroy the works of the devil. How does Jesus destroy the works of the devil today?

3. Ephesians 6 tells about the armor of God. What can we do with the armor of God today?

4. The first stage of battle always takes place in the mind. How can we prepare our mind for battle?

5. How can God use you to reveal His plan and purpose for this generation? For future generations?

EPILOGUE

The Bible is God's Word to us. There is a power in the spoken Word or the rhema of God. There is also a power in the logos or the written Word. In the beginning, God spoke and light existed (Genesis 1:3). In the Book of Genesis, the Lord spoke the world into creation. God's Word has a creative power in it to change things and to change the hearts of men.

When the Word of God is preached, we must choose to act on it. We must be hearers and doers of the Bible. If we hear the Word and do not practice it, Jesus said that we are like a person who builds his house on the sand. Waves will come and waves will go and in time your foundation will be washed away.

For those of us who live on the U.S. coast line, we can understand this example very well. Have you ever stood near the ocean and felt the waves wash the sand from under your feet? Eventually you sink or fall over. In the same manner, if you hear the Word and hear the Word, but never do it, your foundation will be weak and will not be able to support the life you build on it. In order to finish the race of this life, we must commit to be doers of the Word of God.

What have we learned through this book? God is our timeless creator. He is not subject to time as we are. God is the alpha and omega – the first and the last. He sees the beginning and the end.

The power in the spoken word can change a life in a moment. There is a time and a place to release your voice. When Israel was preparing to war over Jericho, we read in Joshua 6:10, "Now Joshua had commanded the people, saying, 'You shall not shout or make any noise with your voice, nor shall a word proceed out of your mouth, until the day I say to you, 'Shout!' Then you shall shout.'" There is a time to release your words and that time is now.

CHAPTER ONE: In the Garden of Eden, the Lord created man in His image. When He did this, God put eternity in our heart. Our body and spirit may be subject to time, but our spirits are eternal. As an eternal being, God has given you a voice.

CHAPTER TWO: We see here where we must write the vision or perish. It is critical to seek after knowledge and wisdom to accomplish our God-given vision. Writing the vision will take us from disorderly or unfocused thoughts to an ordered or structured way of thinking and accomplishing our purpose. Writing the vision gives us focus and allows others to join with us in accomplishing our vision. At this point, we are able to broadcast or publish the vision which should always point to the great things that Jesus has done.

CHAPTER THREE: Vision is an ability to see what God is doing and wants to do in the earth. Cooperating with the Lord will bring success. Our vision or divine ability to see will dictate our actions and our actions will dictate our vision. What we do today will take us to the fulfillment of our vision tomorrow. Allow your God-given vision to direct your life.

CHAPTER FOUR: We are introduced to passion and purpose. Our reason for living should be to do good works. God's purpose for you is to show

His power in and through you. The key to this godly purpose is hidden in your desires. We must not get caught up in spending our lives, but investing it in the purposes of God. What we are doing each day determines our passion.

CHAPTER FIVE: This takes us to a time of discovery. Christopher Columbus was a great discoverer who was directed by the Lord. In 2 Chronicles, we see where the eyes of the Lord move to and fro across the earth. God is not stagnant, but He is alive and moving. God does not change, but His methods and emphasis change. To accomplish God's purposes, we must think outside the box of human reasoning and social correctness.

The people whom God consistently used in the Bible were people of passion, courage and the ability to think and hear new thoughts. The Lord said that our thoughts are not His thoughts and our ways are not His ways. We see that the spirit of the prophet is subject to the prophet. God has equipped us with filters through which we hear and see. We must renew our filters to have the thoughts of God. The Word of God will serve to renew our filters and minds and set the compass for our lives on the true north setting.

CHAPTER SIX: The anointing of God abides. The divine enablement or equipping will remain in the earth. Science teaches that energy cannot be created or destroyed, but it can be transferred.

The spiritual energy to accomplish God's purpose and the vision which He has for your life will not fade from this planet. As we release the anointing God has placed in us, that anointing will continue to produce fruit for the Kingdom of God long after we are gone. The key here is that we must be obedient and diligent to RELEASE. Release is an action verb which requires you to do something.

CHAPTER SEVEN: Jesus knew why He was sent to the world. He knew His purpose. Jesus' purpose was seen by others through what He did and said. The things you do and the words you speak will impact the world around you. We look further into passion and purpose in this chapter. Passion will fuel your vision. The Apostle Paul exhorts us to stir up or activate our gifts, but it is not our job to stir up passion. Passion is a by-product of purpose. As we find our purpose, we will find passion which will be the energy that God uses to make us effective in His Kingdom.

CHAPTER EIGHT: The book of Genesis tells us that mankind was expelled from God's presence in the Garden. Through our sin, we lost access to the Father. In chapter eight of this book, we learn that Jesus came to save and deliver THAT which was lost. When our position and standing in God was restored by what Jesus did on Calvary, we have access to the Kingdom as His children. Jesus came to restore Eden or the place of

God's presence. As we seek God's presence, we will receive a vision of our purpose and have the passion to fulfill the high calling.

CHAPTER NINE: In this chapter, we see the origin and development of the scribe. The scribe has treasures to share with others. This office can see and instruct about things in the past and things in the future. This was a position of authority and influence in the community. In addition to declaring by the Spirit, the scribe began writing things down. The scribe anointing today is housed in the prophetic word. As part of your inheritance, choose to activate the scribe anointing in your life.

CHAPTER TEN: Finally, we see that now is the time. Today is the day of salvation. Today is the day of deliverance. A day is coming when no man will be able to work. After we seek God for our strategy, it's time to put on the armor of God. We have been given powerful weapons to enforce the Lord's victory in the earth. It's time to redeem the time, seize the moment and proclaim the Good News to those in your world.

You can choose to use your voice for good or use it for evil. The overflow of what is in our heart will come out of our mouths in what we speak. The Lord wants us to take our voice and speak His purpose to destroy the works of darkness and uplift the Kingdom of God.

WHERE DO I START?

I did not want to just leave you hanging with what to do next. There is a practical side of releasing your words. Eighty One percent of the population feel they have a book inside them.[1] Here is one plan for you:

- Get alone with God and seek His plan for your life.
- Read the Word and renew your mind.
- Get planted in a local church so you can flourish.
- Actively submit to your local pastor.
- Seek counsel to find safety.
- Refuse to have fear.

- Refuse to doubt.
- Know that God saved you for a purpose and that you are important to Him.
- Do not confuse your ministry with God. Worship God, not the ministry He gave you.
- Journaling can help you examine what's in your heart.
- Write down what God is saying to you.
- Choose to remember what God has done for you.
- Rehearse the victories in your life. Write a memorial.
- Remember that influence is the key to evangelism and impacting others.
- It is the Holy Spirit who convicts the world of sin. It is our job to share the Good News of Jesus Christ who came to save us from our sins and deliver us from unrighteousness.
- Know that God cares more for you than He cares about what you can do; however, out of our love and devotion to the Lord, we have a responsibility to do good works in the Kingdom.

Once you know what God has for you to do, passion and excitement will rise in your spirit. Your road may be difficult at times, but passion will fuel your way and God will give you the grace to reach your destiny. Prepare today to finish the race.

HOW DO I PUBLISH THE GOOD WORKS OF GOD?

Wherever you are or whatever you are doing, you can proclaim God's goodness. God has put you in a place that is occupied by no other. You have a unique ability to fill a hole and meet a need that cannot be touched by another. You may be a policeman or a mother, a teacher or a soldier, but you have a world around you that you are called to influence. Choose to impact those people around you and watch your world change to the glory of God.

Some key thoughts are:

- Formal education is not a pre-requisite for having a testimony. However, determine to do the best with what you have.
- Determine what message God has for you to share with your world. It might be your testimony or a specific message about which God has given you revelation.
- Base your testimony or your revelation on the Word of God. The Bible is a more sure word of prophecy.
- Remember your goal: choose to build up and not tear down.
    - 1 Corinthians 10:23-24 says, *"All things are lawful for me, but not all*

things are helpful; all things are lawful for me, but not all things edify. Let no one seek his own, but each one the other's well-being."

- Ephesians 4:29 reads, *"Let no corrupt communication proceed out of your mouth, but that which is good to the use of edifying, that it may minister grace unto the hearers* (KJV)."

- Write an outline of your message. The goal here is to order your thoughts in some sequence to accomplish a goal. Don't allow legalism in format to choke the life out of what you are doing. If you don't know how to make an outline, find out. If you can't find out, make up one using only numbers or letters.
- Once you have your outline, insert Scriptures and thoughts by topic.
- Use your outline as a map to get you where you want to go.
- A completed manuscript can be viewed as an outline on steroids.
- Don't make your manuscript simply a "word study," but take your goal and keep a Scriptural basis (whether quoted or not.) Expound on the revelation that God has taught you.
- REFUSE to allow excuses to rob you of your purpose.

- If you are intimidated about writing, use an audio recorder and speak into it.
- If you don't have a computer, write it by hand.
- Set time goals in your writing. Try to write a little everyday.
- Smile – it will change your world.
- Go to your pastor with your outline for any input. Your pastor is there for your good. The shepherd of your soul deserves your trust.
- Bounce ideas off your friends and family about what you are writing.
- Choose to walk in love and never to be offended about your work. Being offended is a luxury you cannot afford.
- Be teachable.
- Ask God to set you free from rejection.
- Have fun.
- Always strive to improve and have excellence as your goal.
- Write and rewrite. Then, rewrite again. Make sure that every word you write is useful to your message.
- Once written, allow several friends to proof your manuscript looking for typographical and grammatical errors as well as consistency.
- Allow your manuscript to glorify God.

WHAT IS A PUBLISHER?

A publisher will partner with you to make your testimony or revelation into a book.

- Find a publisher who will protect you and respect your rights. Look for a win-win relationship.
- Don't expect something for nothing in your publishing venture.
- Your publisher will help develop your manuscript into a book.
- Your publisher will make your book accessible to you and others.
- Your publisher will keep your book from ever going out of print.
- Your publisher is your partner for the purposes of God.
- There are a variety of services with which your publisher can assist you.
- Don't forget that no one can sell a book like the author. It's your message and no one believes in it like you do.
- Understand your contractural responsibilities with your publisher.
- Once your book is published, you will be responsible for setting up speaking engagements and author signings. Be sure you understand what publicity your publisher offers.
- Understand your royalty rate and your author purchase price for your book.

Darrell Parsons

is an anointed Bible teacher with profound insight in leadership development and vision casting. His practical application of leadership principles has been obtained through numerous years in the military and in ministry. The Lord has given him a mandate to assist others in reclaiming their voice. Visit www.LDIweb.com for more information on Leadership Development International.

Seminar Topics Include:

- Developing Leaders for Today
- What Makes You Tick - A Look at Your Personality Profile *(certified in the DISC model)*
- Marriage & Family: Cultivating Effective Relationships
- Impacting Your World
- Kingdom Reality Series - Foundational Truths
- Ten Effective Christian Attitudes
- Certified in teaching Stephen Covey's *7 **Habits of Highly Effective People***

Speaking invitations may be e-mailed to Darrell@LDIweb.com.

ORDER TODAY

PORTRAIT OF A PASTOR'S HEART
A Manual on Caring for the Sheep
by Bishop Gerald Doggett

This book is a must for pastors, elders, students & laymen who want to learn how to care for the flock of God. Bishop Gerald Doggett paints a rare and intimate portrait of a pastor's heart after having served congregations for over thirty years. He covers TOPICS such as: Spirit of a Finisher, The Necessity of the Divine Call and A Beautiful Portrait of Preparation. Order your copy today for only $12.95 + $3 S/H.

RELEASE YOUR WORDS IMPACT YOUR WORLD
by Darrell Parsons

Your words can make a difference! God has done something in the life of every believer. He has placed treasures inside you that He wants to use to touch hearts and minds. The Lord wants to use you to touch your world! It's time to release your words to impact your world. The vision is for the appointed time and that time is now! Order your copy today for only $9.95 + $3 S/H.

www.ParsonsPublishingHouse.com

Printed in the United States
82080LV00002B/13-216

9 781602 730007